The Power to Become!

By: Apostle Larry D. Sims, D. Min.

No part of this publication may be reproduced or transmitted in any form or by any means, mechanical or electronic, including photocopying for recording, or by any information storage and retrieval system, without express written permission from the author.

ISBN-13: 978-1-7322740-0-6

ISBN-10: 1-7322740-0-2

Printed in the U.S.A.

First Edition

The Power to Become!

By: Apostle Larry D. Sims, D. Min.

Dedication

I would like to dedicate this book to:

First, To My Lord and Savior Jesus Christ for His Glory!

To my Grandparents

The Late Mother Alveta Bell Williams - Hall
Mother Charlie Mae Sims
Mother Omega Hill
Mrs. Minne Williams
The Late Amos Williams, Sr.
The Late George Bankston
The Late Winter Hall

And to my Leaders & Mentors
Past & Present
__(Alphabetized by Senior Leaders First Name)__

Rev. Amos E. & The Late Lady Christine Williams, Sr.
Archbishop C. W. & Mother Mary Maddox
Bishop Elijah & Dr. Victoria Gray
The Late Dr. Jerry & Elder B. J. (Gray) Blackman
Apostle Laura & Mr. Dale "Daddy" Thompson
The Late Rev. Paul L. Boswell & Lady Betty Boswell
The Late Bishop Paul & Pastor Emma White
Apostles Ronnie & Veronica Johnson
Bishop Ronnie & Lady Vivian Powell
Bishop Thomas D. & Lady Vickie Strong

Acknowledgements & Thanks

I have to first give honor to God who is the head of my life. Without Him none of this would be possible. I am in awe that He would trust me with such an assignment. I will never deserve it! But He chooses to use me in spite of me.

Next, I must thank my wife Adrean. She has been there making sacrifices while I'm up late at night writing, on the phone with my editor and branding coach and doing ministry in general. She didn't complain ... much ... (LOL!) even though she would prefer me to be there in bed with her. No one really knows the sacrifice of a minister's spouse and the selflessness that they have to have in order to be married to the preacher/pastor. Thank You Bae! I Love you to life!

To my Mom, Rosa, thank you for what you instilled in me. You introduced and gave me back to God. You never told me I couldn't do anything God said do. You have been one of my biggest supporters even sometimes when I was a handful ... Lol! Thank you and know that I love you! Your sacrifices have not gone unnoticed and they were not in vain.

To my second Mom, Linda, thank you for your love and support over the years. You have been there pushing and encouraging me even when you didn't have to. So many have a different experience and outlook when it comes to their "step" parent, but because of your heart of love, I'm blessed to call you Mom and blood couldn't make us closer.

To my Dad, Donell, thank you for the things you have done and for your love and support over the years. We haven't always seen eye-to-eye, but you have never given up on me. I love you and thank God for you. Thank you for being my Dad!

To my only blood sister, Tasia, I love you Sis! Thanks for all the love and support you have given me over the years. I know you love to hear me sing so hopefully the CD is coming next ... LOL! We'll just have to see what God has up His sleeve.

To my brother, Clarence, words cannot express my gratitude for the love and support you have given me. This project would still be an idea in my head if it were not for you pushing and challenging me. Thanks for the brainstorming sessions, opening up your office for me to use when needed, for the conversations and the encouragement when I wanted to give up and quit. I am honored to call you my brother and blood couldn't make us closer.

To my family ... thank you for your love and support!

To my ministry/church family ... thank you all for your love and support! Thank you for believing in me sometimes when I didn't believe in myself. You all PUSH me and keep me going. I love you all to life!

And to my editor and coach Renée Purdie, thanks. You challenged me to get this done in what honestly I thought was an impossible timeline and though we had to extend it two weeks, you stayed on me and now it is done! PRAISE THE LORD! I have to get Twanna something for introducing us ... LOL!

And to anyone and everyone who has played a part in my life ... Thank You!!!

Table of Contents

The Foreword

The POWER TO BECOME is designed to show us exactly who we are in Christ. When we understand who God has called us to be, then we will stand to be true pillars and mantle keepers for the Kingdom. The Power to Become teaches us real sonship, which is more than a future inheritance; it is a lifetime of residual and perpetual benefits.

The eighty-fourth chapter of Psalms verse eleven declares: "For the Lord God is a sun and shield: The Lord bestows grace and favor and honor; no good thing will He withhold from those who walk uprightly."

When we as true sons and daughters walk upright before our God, we will receive simply because of our obedience to Him. God desires the very best for us, but it is vital to the Kingdom that we become the Sons and Daughters he designed us to be.

The POWER TO BECOME takes away all excuses, situations and circumstances. We must understand that God designed us to fulfill our purpose and carry out His destiny for our lives. God is so thoughtful in the areas that concern us. We must realize that our blessings don't stop when our life expires on this side; they leave a legacy for generations to pattern themselves by.

Let us embrace the POWER TO BECOME exactly who GOD DESIRES US TO BE!

In His name and for His Sake,

Dr. Laura M. Thompson

Introduction

In today's world, there is so much going on pulling at us from every side. When was the last time you took time to invest in your dreams and goals? How long have you said, "I'm going to write that book this year!" or "I'm going to start my business!"

This book will challenge you to press pass all of your excuses and fears to do what needs to be done to fulfill your dreams, goals, and aspirations and ultimately your God-given assignment. This book is designed to challenge the source of your fear, the lies from your past, and the untapped ability locked on the inside of you waiting to be released.

I, too, have been where you are. I have wanted to write a book for more than 10 years, but I've made excuses and allowed fear to keep me from doing it. After applying the principles in this book and getting a good nudge from the Lord, *The Power to Become* was birthed!

I have preached the principles in this book for many years and people have given testimony of how it has changed their outlook and their lives. The great thing about this book is it's simple and easy to read. You can read it today and start applying the principles today. If you read this book and begin to apply the principles to your life, I promise you will never be the same! You will be ready to launch out into the deep and go for ALL that God has promised you.

The majority of the excuses and fears we allow to keep us from stepping out and doing what we are called to do are lies that we embrace to keep us where we are, in a place of discontentment and unfulfillment. Please don't be the one that says I'll get it later or I'll read it later. Don't waste another year, month, week, day, hour, minute, or even second holding on to those excuses, fears, and roadblocks, keeping you from accomplishing your dreams, goals, and aspirations! Be the one that says, "I stepped out; I did it, and I'm glad I did!" Take back control of your life, and do it TODAY!

The lessons and principles you're about to read have been proven time and time again. All you have to do is read and apply these principles to your life by doing the necessary work. Each chapter will challenge you and encourage you to become the "Best You" God has created you to be.

Chapter 1

"It's Time for Change!"

*And the Lord said unto Samuel, How long wilt thou
mourn for Saul, seeing I have rejected him from
reigning over Israel? fill thine horn with oil, and go,
I will send thee to Jesse the Beth-lehemite: for I
have provided me a king among his sons.*

1 Samuel 16:1

We see it; we feel it and we know it … It's time for change. A few definitions for change are:

a) to become different
b) to become transformed or converted
c) to switch or to make an exchange

Though there are more, these stick out the most and deal most with the subject at hand. If we were to be honest, we know a lot of things that need to be different, transformed and/or converted.

There are things in every area of our lives that need some form of change and transformation: in our homes, in our families, on our job, in our churches and even in our communities. But like most people, we sit back and wait for someone else to change things. It's easier to pass the buck and place the burden of responsibility on someone else rather that stepping up to the challenge and taking on the task ourselves.

In many cases, we have to realize that the thing that irritates us is the thing that we are called to handle. If you get frustrated at the injustice happening in your community, perhaps you need to speak out about it or organize a group to help deal with it in a peaceful, productive manner that will effect change. If you go to a church and you see there is nothing going on for the young people and you have a heart to see young people involved and engaged in the church, perhaps you're called to work with the youth ministry. Even if it's just for a season or until the permanent person shows up, you can be the change.

If you get frustrated because you see your pastor overworked and doing more than necessary, perhaps you need to step up and take some weight off him/her so they can focus more on the Word and work of the ministry. You may even be called to help form groups to help enhance the ministry and facilitate the pastor's vision and the church's mission. Even on your job, you may see something that needs to be addressed or a procedure that could be better implemented. You can take the initiative, following protocol, to submit your idea or suggestion.

I know you may say, "I'm nobody. No one cares about what I think. I'm just one person and my voice doesn't count." This can't be further from the truth. There are so many great inventions and luxuries we have today because someone dared to go against the normal way of doing things.

Your decision to step out and address the issue and pursue change could very well be the catalyst that brings the conversion, difference and transformation needed to change your family, your church, your community and even the world. When you are called to be great, no matter how much you want to sit on the sidelines and be a spectator, you can't hide because God will send for you. As we see in the story of David, he was minding his own business, watching his father's sheep when he was called and anointed to be the king of Israel.

When God rejected King Saul and chose David, He sent the Prophet Samuel to anoint him to be the next king of Israel. Even when David's father neglected to call him in when Prophet Samuel told him to bring all his sons before him, God did not let the father's disregard for David or Prophet Samuel's fleshly outlook to get in the way of His plan. In the end, Jesse, David's Father, had to go get David,

From a spiritual standpoint, we must understand that there is and has been a changing of the guard. There are leaders both naturally and spiritually that God has shifted and/or rejected that may be physically holding the position, but the anointing has been removed. This is not to say that every person has committed sin and been rejected by God; however, some have been shifted and called to another place, but someone has to take their place. Many of them know their time is up. Some are waiting for their replacement to get prepared and show up. Others are bitter and reprobate, trying to hold on to a place they have been rejected from. The fact of the matter is, you have to make a decision, "Am I going to continue to sit, hoping and wishing, or am I going to get up and embrace the journey ahead and become who God has created me to be?"

It is important to make the decision about what you're going to do because based on this decision you can then begin to make plans to achieve your goal. It is important to set realistic, reachable steps to reach your goal. Setting these staps keeps you focused, on-track, and accountable.

Now let's begin... List at least three (3) changes you would like to see made. This can be for yourself, your home, your job/business, your church, your community and/or all five (5). Use a separate sheet of paper if needed.

_____

_____

_____

_____

_____

Now think about and list at least two (2) ways you can initiate each thing you would like to see changed. Don't overthink it and don't focus on the total process. Take it one step at a time.

_____

_____

_____

_____

_____

Chapter 2

"You Were Anointed For This!"

And he sent, and brought him in. Now he was ruddy,
and withal of a beautiful countenance, and goodly
to look to. And the Lord said, Arise, anoint him: for
this is he.

1 Samuel 16:12

N o matter how much you want to be normal,
you're not normal. You were not created to
be normal, and fortunately, you will NEVER

be normal. You can try to hide, but you will always stick out like a sore thumb.

When I was younger, I wanted to fit in with everybody else, so I tried to dress like them and even went to a party with them. While at the party, I was dancing and acting like everyone else. I even chose to speak like everyone else and use profanity. After a few hours had passed, I was just sitting there when someone walked up to me that I didn't even know and they asked me, "What are you doing here? You know you don't belong here!" I felt so bad and immediately the conviction of the Holy Spirit fell on me. The rest of the night I was miserable, but I had to stay until my ride was ready to leave and take me home.

Ever since I can remember, I've always been told that I was going to be a preacher. That definitely wasn't something I wanted or prayed for. My personal desire was and still is to sing. I have always loved music. If I was asked what I wanted to do when I grew up, the answer would be a singer. I saw myself traveling the world, singing at concerts and recording CDs. This was my desire, but God had somewhat of a different plan.

Though my situation is a lot different from his, I can somewhat relate to David. See, I've always been the different one. I was different from all the other kids including my cousins. The Lord has had his hand on my life from a very young age. I remember when I received my call from God at the age of six years old. Though I was too young to understand it, I do remember the experience. Some years later at the age of ten, I received the call again. At the time, I was reluctant because of my age and the fact I knew I was different. I had seen the effects my being "Different" had on my ability to make friends and I didn't want to add another friend repellent.

After my mom and step-dad decided to move us to a new city, I was invited to a church I had never been to before. I was walking around to place my offering in the offering plate when the pastor called me out. I tried to ignore him, but he called me up to the front and prophesied that it was time for me to stop running from God because I was going to preach. Though I knew he was telling the truth, my flesh was like, "How he going to call me out like that; he doesn't even know me!"

After I got off the floor from being slayed in the Holy Ghost, I went home and cried for a week, the rest is history. If you know me, you know I'm a preacher and have been for twenty-five plus years now. The moral of this story is … when God wants to use you, you can try to hide, but He will get you. Just ask Jonah.

Though you may be looked over and may feel inadequate, remember, David was not in the original line-up when Jesse presented his sons. The Prophet Samuel asked after seeing all the sons Jesse presented, "Are these all your children?" The answer was, of course, no. Similarly, when it's your season and your time, nothing and no one can stop you or take your place. They may have counted you out and said you're too young, you're too old, you don't have the "right" look, you don't have the education and you don't know the right people. But you can rest in the fact that while you may not be the popular choice, you are God's choice and that's all that matters!

Now I want you to repeat and believe the following confession:

I am Who God says I am!

I can do what God says I can do!

I will be ALL that God created me to be!

I accept God's Will for my life!

I embrace God's Will for my life!

I walk in God's Will for my life!

Repeat and Declare this over your life daily!

Chapter 3

"Stay In The Process!"

But David went and returned from Saul to feed his
father's sheep at Bethlehem.

1 Samuel 17:15

One of the greatest enemies of our destiny—
aside from negative self-perception—is the
lack of patience to walk out our process. The
enemy tells us because it didn't happen immediately
and doesn't happen in the timeframe we think it
should happen that God has forgotten about us or
He's not going to do it for us. This many times
causes frustration and provokes us to move and try
to make it happen ourselves. This is one of the
greatest mistakes that we can make, and if we are

not careful, it could cause us to abort our destiny and forfeit our purpose. You have to understand that your process prepares, propels, and positions you for purpose.

David gives us a great example of the benefits of staying in our process. After being anointed to be the next King of Israel, David went back to watching the sheep. Stop a minute and think about that. We must understand the anointing comes because of the assignment and call, but just because you are anointed, doesn't mean you are ready. There is more that God wants to show you and develop in you to prepare you and qualify you for your place of purpose. There were experiences that David had while watching the sheep that prepared him for the upcoming battle he would face, and had he not had the shepherd experience, perhaps he would not have been prepared for the upcoming challenge.

Do not allow people or your own emotions to cause you to make a premature move. Though the purpose of God can still be fulfilled in your life, it can prolong the manifestation and even cause you to forfeit blessings and opportunities. This can be seen later in David's life when he was rejected to build the temple because of the blood that was on his hands from the murder of Bathsheba's husband, Uriah.

Another thing to remember is you cannot judge your process by someone else's process. They could have started and been in their process many years before you even encountered them. Also understand they may not be called to where you are called, and thus, your process will be different.

I can remember going to a restaurant one time and placing my order. Moments later, another group of people were seated, and their order was taken. After a while had passed, I saw the table seated after us was being served. Upset and feeling like we had been overlooked, we called the server and expressed our dissatisfaction with not being served before the table seated after us. She then apologized and explained that it wasn't that we were being overlooked, it was just that what we ordered takes longer to prepare. We'd ordered some thick cut steaks that we wanted medium well to well done; whereas, the table seated after us only ordered chicken fingers, appetizers, and salads.

The person you're comparing yourself to may be in a totally different arena that calls for a totally different process. Also, you can't judge success by the first glance because fast growth doesn't always mean sustained growth. As a pastor and church leader, I notice the speed at which some new ministries grow. And as a church planter, I have noticed the struggle sometimes I have to grow the ministry versus some of my counterparts and co-laborers in the gospel. Honestly, there has been times where I was discouraged and felt like there was something wrong with me as a leader. Then God would say, "Look closer and look deeper." Everything that's big isn't healthy; sometimes it's just swelling. Indeed, some of those same churches that I almost allowed to get me off focus aren't even in existence today.

We must learn to trust the process of God and know that just because it is not (yet) your time, it doesn't mean it is not your turn. When you go to the doctor and you sign in, it puts you in line to be seen by the doctor. When you're next in line, no matter how many or who signs in, you're next. They may be seeing other patients already or simply be getting the room together for you. Either way, you're next because it's still your turn. All you have to do is allow the process to take its course.

Chapter 4

"Follow Instructions!"

And David rose up early in the morning, and left the sheep with a keeper, and took, and went, as Jesse had commanded him; and he came to the trench, as the host was going forth to the fight, and shouted for the battle.

1 Samuel 17:20

This chapter is one that will challenge your flesh. We live in a world where rebellion is on the rise. Everyone seems to think that they don't need anyone else and that they can make it on

21

their own. This further breeds a lack of respect for leadership and authority.

We use terms like mentor, spiritual father, leader and pastor, just to name a few, so loosely. I Corinthians 4:15 (KJV) says, "For though ye have ten thousand instructors in Christ, yet *have ye* not many fathers: for in Christ Jesus I have begotten you through the gospel." The fact is we often submit ourselves to people for what they can give us rather than for what they can impart in us. We seek out platforms, personalities and resources rather than someone that will cover, impart and protect our soul and destiny.

In my early years of ministry, I was told that you need three types of people in your life. First, you need someone to look up to. This is an authority figure to instruct, guide, and challenge you. Next, you need someone on your level as an equal. These are your peers. They are people that you can relate to and perhaps, they can help you along your journey to destiny. And lastly, you need someone under you. This would be someone that you mentor, help, challenge, and/or instruct.

With all of this said, we must make sure that we do not miss proper instruction. No matter how great you are, you need to have someone that you can submit your greatness to. You need someone that can call you to the carpet when you are wrong and in error that you genuinely respect, honor, and submit to. Our ability to be great leaders is tested in our ability to be great followers. It is truthfully said, "Leaders aren't made: they are born." However, they are only effective through proper training and application.

I am a legitimately consecrated bishop and affirmed apostle in the Lord's church. I have been preaching the gospel of Jesus Christ for more than 25 years, yet I have Leaders and mentors that I submit to for training, instruction and impartation. When we look at this from a natural standpoint, we see that no matter how old you get, you can still get wisdom and instruction from your parents and grandparents. This is true because you never outgrow learning and gaining wisdom.

We see David as a great example of being obedient and following instructions. Because of his obedience to watch his father's sheep, he had valuable experiences that prepared him for a future opportunity. Furthermore, it also positioned him to receive the opportunity. His obedience and following the instruction of his father caused him to be present at the battle at the proper time to hear what he needed to hear and see what he needed to see. Perhaps, if he had not gone to take his brothers food as his father instructed him, he would have missed seeing Goliath and hearing what the soldiers had to say. He would have missed the opportunity to say what he said that caused King Saul to send for him. Following this, David's obedience also caused him to have favor with King Saul.

Many times, we look for direct instruction telling us something related to our agenda; however, sometimes the simple act of obedience can cause us to have the greatest opportunities of our lives. I can remember one time that obedience caused a door to open for me.

Many years ago, I was invited to minister at a Healing and Deliverance Crusade in a neighboring city. I had the task of preaching some nights and leading praise & worship on the other nights. Early in the crusade, the crowds began to dwindle, and needless to say, I wasn't being compensated for my travels. At the time, I had an older Cadillac that was horrible on gas. It was about three nights before the end of the crusade, and I didn't have the gas money to go to the crusade. My Mom came home and asked why I wasn't dressed. I told her about the gas situation. A few minutes later, she walked in and gave me money for gas. Knowing our financial situation, I said, "No, you need this more than I need to go to this crusade." She preceded to tell me, "No, take it! I feel like you need to go tonight." After going back and forth for a moment, I said, "OK, I'll go." I arrived, late of course. I led worship and sat down. After the service, the host invited me to dinner, and I was ecstatic. That was the first sign of any compensation I'd received the entire crusade. I got to the restaurant, and I was informed that the host's Presiding Bishop would be joining us ... and he was in the service. By the end of dinner, I was booked for an international crusade to be held on the Island of Bermuda, and I would be on the stage with gospel great, Alvin Slaughter from TBN. Seriously?!

Had I not obeyed my Mother and went to the crusade that night, I would have missed a great opportunity. I am still connected with the Presiding Bishop I met that night. I am a part of the Executive Board of Bishops in his organization. All of this happened from one act of obedience. You might not like it, or think it's irrelevant, but make sure you receive instructions and are obedient. I Samuel 15:22 states, "And Samuel said, Hath the Lord *as great* delight in burnt offerings and sacrifices, as in obeying the voice of the Lord? Behold, to obey *is* better than sacrifice, *and* to hearken than the fat of rams." Remember no matter how much you give, help and sacrifice for others in the name of God, or for a good cause, there is no greater blessing or reward than that received from obedience.

Chapter Application

List at least three (3) individuals on each level presently in your life:

Leaders/Mentors

1. _____

2. _____

3. _____

4. _____

5. _____

Peers/Equals

1. _____

2. _____

3. _____

4. _____

5. _____

The Power to Become

Mentees/Students

1. _____

2. _____

3. _____

4. _____

5. _____

Chapter 5

"It's NOT About You!"

23 And as he talked with them, behold, there came up the champion, the Philistine of Gath, Goliath by name, out of the armies of the Philistines, and spake according to the same words: and David heard them.

24 And all the men of Israel, when they saw the man, fled from him, and were sore afraid.

25 And the men of Israel said, Have ye seen this man that is come up? surely to defy Israel is he

The Power to Become
come up: and it shall be, that the man who killeth him, the king will enrich him with great riches, and will give him his daughter, and make his father's house free in Israel.

1 Samuel 17:23-25

What are you anointed and/or gifted to do? Can you sing? Preach? Pray? Are you good in business? Are you good in mathematics, social science, English? Are you a good literary writer or songwriter? Perhaps you're a great administrator.

What is that thing you go to bed dreaming about and wake up in the morning thinking about?

What vision has the Lord given you?

Take a brief moment and list at least three things you're anointed/gifted to do:

1. _____

2. _____

3. _____

4. _____

5. _____

I'm sure you have a lot of goals, dreams and desires to use your gifts. Perhaps you plan on making a living using these gifts one day, if you're not already doing so. I'm also sure you have an array of emotions that come along with these dreams and desires, but no matter where you are in your journey, you must remember that it's NOT about you!

Too many times we get caught up in our abilities and talents that we lose focus on the ultimate purpose which is to affect others. Yes, our abilities and talents may yield certain benefits and amenities, but we must remember the reason for our gifts. Your ability to preach and/or sing is to minister to others so they can experience God in a way that draws them closer to Him so they can either start a relationship with Him or strengthen their existing one. If you're a business owner or product creator, your business/product is not just for you. It's to help others which causes people to purchase and patronize. No matter how anointed you are, without an audience to minister to, it's a waste. No matter how great a business/product you have, if you don't have customers, it's simply a useless idea.

In the story of David, we see that he looked at the greater cause, the safety of his people. His desire and decision to pursue the giant, Goliath, was more than a desire to look good before people, though it was a benefit.

When on your journey to destiny, you have to look beyond the glitz, glam, and lights and look for the great cause and call. Benefits and popularity change regularly. Look at Jesus! One week they were crying, "Hosanna!" (Hosanna means Savior.) And the very next week, the same people were screaming: "Crucify him!" So, don't be moved by the hype! As quickly as they lift you up, they will pull you back down even quicker.

Another thing that may not sit right with you was also showed by Jesus dying for the same people who were crying out for his blood. You do not have the right to say who your gift is for. God may cause you to minister to the very one that hurt you or tried to kill you. You may have to minister to the very one God told you that you're going to replace. After being anointed king, David had to go minister unto Saul, even when he tried to kill him.

We also have to continually walk in a place of humility, so that we don't allow the spirit of pride to cause us to miss our blessings and not fulfill our purpose. Pride and fear are two of the biggest killers of Destiny and Purpose. Please kill "IT" before it kills you!

For some, I know you may be scared or just don't want to do it, but there are people waiting on you to release what's inside of you. You may be the one that God wants to use to pull them out of what they are in and even push them to the place they need to be in their journey to destiny. Some people you're called to help may not even know they need help until they come in contact with you. They may be stuck and not even know they are stuck. Your gift and/or ability could be the next big thing to affect the world. So even through fear and doubt, you have to remember: It's Not About You!

Chapter 6

"Pay Attention!"

*And David spake to the men that stood by him,
saying, What shall be done to the man that killeth
this Philistine, and taketh away the reproach from
Israel? for who is this uncircumcised Philistine, that
he should defy the armies of the living God?*

1 Samuel 17:26

It is simple common sense that you will gravitate in the direction of your focus. I was driving some years ago when I saw an event happening a ways off from me to my right. I was so engulfed in being nosey trying to see what was going on until I noticed the car was about to go off the road in the direction I was looking. I have noticed this while walking as well.

It is a natural thing to look at the things around us; however, we must make sure that we are not just looking at one thing, but paying attention to everything around us. There are a lot of things that can be learned, avoided, and attained simply by paying attention.

Our main focus should be on the destination or goal we are trying to achieve. We should strategically plan and focus our actions in line with our purpose and destiny all the while paying attention to our surroundings. We have to pay attention to people, places, and things.

On our journey to destiny, many types of people will come into our life. Some people are lifetime fixtures. They aren't going anywhere. These people are your "ride or die" people. They will be there through the good, bad, ugly and indifferent.

Then there are your seasonal people. These are the people that will only be in your life for a short time. Though they aren't life timers, they are still important and necessary. You have to be careful when dealing with seasonal people. You don't want to keep them too long because then it becomes toxic. When someone's season is up ... let them go! It doesn't mean they are bad people or they don't love you, but they have fulfilled their purpose and it's time for them to move on.

Next is what I like to call "the distractions." These people come in our lives to distract us and get us off focus. You have to be really careful with these people because they look attractive and many times offer what you seem to be missing and needing, but their assignment is to get us off focus and ultimately miss our destiny and purpose. They come in offering flattery and promising the world. Many times, they come when we are at a low point and feeling discouraged. Watch who you talk to. Every ear isn't an ear of comfort. You could be giving your enemy the ammo to take you out!

When dealing with people, you definitely have to watch their actions and motives. You can't be so desperate for help and/or attention that you allow the wrong people to infiltrate your life. If you watch and pay attention, the true motives of individuals will always show up. People always tell you who they are; it's up to you to listen.

Next you have to pay attention to the place you are in. What's going on? Is it productive or unproductive? Is it helping or hurting you? Are you growing, stagnated or dying? What opportunities are available to you? You should never stay or engage in a place that isn't producing. Your time and resources are too valuable to waste it with people, places and things that don't value you and/or add value to you.

No matter where you are, you should look for opportunity for advancement. As we look at the story of David, we see that as he went to obey his father's instructions to take his brothers food, he was watching and listening to what was going on. Because of this, he was able to see an opportunity that would change his life forever. Pay attention and don't miss any moments or opportunities that could change your life and the lives of those connected to you.

Can you identify any distractions present in your life at this time and any that seem to cycle in and out at varying times and seasons?

_____

_____

_____

_____

_____

_____

What changes can you make and things can you do to stop these distractions and hindrances?

_____

_____

_____

_____

_____

_____

_____

Chapter 7

"Stay Focused!"

29 And David said, What have I now done? Is there
not a cause?
30 And he turned from him toward another, and
spake after the same manner: and the people
answered him again after the former manner.

1 Samuel 17:29-30

On our journey to our place of promise, we
have a lot of distractions. These distractions,

if not dealt with properly, can cause us to miss reaching our place of promise or greatly delay it. We have to be very careful who and what we allow in our lives because if they are not helping to push us where we need to go, it's a distraction.

Distractions can come in many forms and sometimes appear to be good things. We must understand every "good" thing is not a God thing. I want you to take a moment and ask yourself, "What is distracting me from moving forward, reaching my goals and fulfilling my purpose?" Please write it down. Seeing things in black and white helps us clarify things.

_____

_____

_____

_____

_____

_____

_____

_____

Now decide, "How am I going to change this?"

_____

_____

_____

_____

_____

_____

_____

_____

_____

_____

_____

_____

_____

_____

I know you may be saying, "Why is this so important?" This is important because if you never identify the issue and correct it, you will never progress and ultimately you will never reach your place of promise. We have to learn to STAY FOCUSED!

One definition of focus is a central point, as of attraction, attention, or activity. What you invest in is where you get your return if one is yielded. You can't plant apple seeds and expect to get an orange tree. You can't plant a garden in Alabama and expect to harvest in Georgia. You have to focus all your energy, tools and talents toward your goal. If you desire to open a business, at least 90% of your day should be geared and directed to that.

I know you may say, but there is more to life than working on my business! What about my job? My family? My friends? That is true to a point; however, you have to prioritize everything in your life and keep it in perspective. Even with that said, I still say 90% of your day should be geared toward you reaching your desired goal. Everyone around you should know the ultimate goal you're shooting for. Anyone that gives you a moment of their time should walk away knowing where your heart is.

Anyone that knows me knows I LOVE MINISTRY. In fact, even if you don't know me, if you talk with me long enough, you'll realize I love and desire to do ministry, and that's the way it should be. It is my passion. It's what I desire to do 24/8, and yes, I know it's 24/7, but I love doing ministry so much that I'm prepared to add an extra dimension to mathematics! I know that my immediate family is called to ministry. Everyone may not be a preacher in the pulpit, but they all will work in some form of ministry. Even most of the purchases I make are made with ministry in mind.

Successful people don't waste time worrying about what someone else is doing because they are too busy doing what they do and being successful. The more you waste time looking at and comparing yourself to others, the longer you're going to stay in the place you are. Also, stop listening to the chatter about you. The fact of the matter is, people are going to talk about you no matter what. If you're doing well, they are going to talk, and if you are doing poorly, they are going to talk.

Sometimes those closest to you may not understand the call and anointing on your life, but you have to stay focused. Habakkuk 2:3 lets us know that the vision is for an appointed time and though it tarries, we are to wait for it because it shall speak and not lie. We see in the story of David that his brother tried to discourage him when he inquired about the reward for killing the Philistine, but he stayed focused. He spoke to those around him until his words made it all the way to King Saul.

When you know your assignment/goal, that has to be your focus and motivation. You have to look at everything as a tool or resource to help get you to your place of purpose. Your job is just a temporary resource to produce seed and meet your current level of need. Your current home is just a stepping stone to prepare you for the promised place. Though everything may not go as you desire, you have to know in whom you believe and His ability to bring it to pass.

So, let the haters hate and the doubters doubt. You stay focused and keep moving forward. Don't listen or worry about the naysayers. Think about those who you are going to help and impact. Drown out the noise and focus because God's purpose is calling!

What is your current focus?

_____

_____

_____

_____

Chapter 8

"Be YOU!"

31 And when the words were heard which David spake, they rehearsed them before Saul: and he sent for him.

32 And David said to Saul, Let no man's heart fail because of him; thy servant will go and fight with this Philistine.

1 Samuel 17:31-32

A s we are on the journey to our purpose, it causes us to go down self-discovery lane.

44

During this time when we are trying to find ourselves and our niche, it is easy to compare ourselves to others and even try to mimic them in our own life. Though it is okay to glean and take nuggets from others, you should never try to be or operate like someone else. God made you an original!

It is okay to be you and be confident in who God has created you to be, but there is a difference between being confident and cocky. Confidence says, "I know the abilities God placed in me, and I trust that He has empowered me to do what I do. It doesn't make me better than anyone else, and I can celebrate the gift of God in you while accepting the gift of God in me." Cocky says, "I'm better than everyone else, and I'm the only one that can do it. It's all about me!" Never be cocky because it's not about you!

There are many benefits and power in being you! God made you for a purpose, and no one else can take your place. The reason you should only be you is because no one can beat you being you. You have a tailor-made assignment that only you can fulfill. In order to have lasting success, you have to be and do you. There is a favor and a grace that comes when you operate in your anointing and call. There is even a peace for those who are operating in their own lane. The Bible states in Proverbs 16:7 (KJV): "When a man's ways please the Lord, he maketh even his enemies to be at peace with him." You don't have to pretend or wear a mask to please people. You can just be wo you are and do what you are called to do.

We see in the life of David that he was confident in who he was and who God called him to be. He spoke with such confidence and assurance to the point that his words reached King Saul and moved him so much that he called for David. When invited to speak with the king, David again walked in with confidence, not just in his ability to go against the enemy, but in the assurance and power of his God.

When you know your anointing, assignment and call, there is no need to be afraid or timid when the time comes for you to operate in it. Being truthful and transparent, there should be some godly fear/concern in that you want to make sure you are pleasing to God and doing what he wants you to do, but it should not be a paralyzing, terrifying fear.

*For God hath not given us the spirit of fear;
but of power and of love, and of a sound mind.*
2 Timothy 1:7

David received favor from King Saul because of his confidence—and doing what he promised to do. You DO NOT have to apologize for being who you are! God has called us all and given us abilities, anointings and talents, but it up to us to use them.

Though our anointing and gifts may be different, they all work to complement each other and ultimately benefit the Kingdom of God. Learn to be you, accept you and do you because you are a vital part of the Kingdom and we need YOU!

Now I want you to repeat and believe the following confessions daily:

- o I am fearfully and wonderfully made in the image and likeness of God!

- o I am called, chosen and anointed for such a time at this to **You Fill in the Blank**!

- o I have everything I need to accomplish my call, my goals and my assignment.

- o I lack nothing because God supplies all my needs.

- o I do not fear doing what God has called me to do because I know He is with me and shall give me the strength and ability to do it!

- o I declare and decree that EVERY plot, plan, scheme, and working of the enemy is cancelled and brought to naught in Jesus's Name!

o I shall accomplish my assignment in Jesus's Name!

o I come into agreement with God's Will for my life.

o I declare and decree all of these things to be so NOW in the Mighty, Powerful and Matchless Name of Jesus Christ! And It Is So!

Chapter 9

"Don't Forget!"

34 And David said unto Saul, Thy servant kept his father's sheep, and there came a lion, and a bear, and took a lamb out of the flock:

35 And I went out after him, and smote him, and delivered it out of his mouth: and when he arose against me, I caught him by his beard, and smote him, and slew him.

36 Thy servant slew both the lion and the bear: and this uncircumcised Philistine shall be as one of them, seeing he hath defied the armies of the living God.

37 David said moreover, The Lord that delivered me out of the paw of the lion, and out of the paw of the bear, he will deliver me out of the hand of this Philistine. And Saul said unto David, Go, and the Lord be with thee.

1 Samuel 17:34-37

As we travel throughout our life and journey, we are going to have many experiences, some good and some not so pleasant. Through all that happens, it is important that you do not forget where you've come from and what you've been through. It is said that our life experiences make us who and what we are. I don't totally agree with this, but I'll say our life experiences can shape who we are based on how we look at them and use them in our future. Many of us have stories to tell that aren't glamorous. We have things in our past that we aren't proud of whether it came by choice or by force. But at the end of the day, you have to ask yourself: What am I going to do with it? No matter what happened to you, the fact is if you're reading this book … You made it!

God saw fit to allow you to go through that thing. More importantly, He gave you enough strength and the ability to come out with your right mind and the opportunity to move on. That's a testimony all by itself. There are others that went through less and lost their mind and are in a mental institution or worse, committed suicide.

I know you may be hurt and don't fully understand why you had to go through it, but know Romans 8:28 lets us know that "ALL things work together for good to them that love God, to them who are the called according to His purpose."

We have to come to the place that we truly trust and know the God we serve. He has given us all promises that we must hold fast to. We have to know that no matter what we face, His Word is true, and it's going to come to pass. If He did it before, He can do it again. He's the same yesterday, today, and forevermore. He changes not!

As we face new obstacles on our journey to destiny, we have to remember the past victories that God has caused us to win. The Bible declares in Revelation 12:11: "And they overcame him by the blood of the Lamb, and by the word of their testimony." The power of our testimony gives us strength through the hard times and reminds us that God is able! He's willing and He will bring us through the present challenge we are facing.

We see David in I Samuel 17:34-35 remembering and sharing his testimony of having to come up against a lion and a bear that came to take one of his father's sheep. God gave him the ability and power to overcome the lion and the bear, delivering the sheep back into the fold. David had confidence that he would be able to overcome the Philistine enemy because God had delivered him before from the lion and the bear. He had such confidence that he was able to convince the king to allow him to go up against the Philistine.

Your testimony should be so powerful and transformative that it causes the hearer to have a totally different outlook and a greater trust in God. It should be so moving that if they don't know God, they want to know him after hearing your testimony. Your testimony is a testament of the power and ability of God.

Sharing your testimony often requires you to forgive and let go of the past. You have a choice. You can look at your past experiences and test and harbor anger, hate, and unforgiveness, or you can accept what happened, forgive the perpetrators, thank God you made it and move on. Holding on to hate only hinders you because the other people involved have moved on (one way or the other). Some have forgotten what they did and others are dead and gone.

There are people that need to hear your story. They are in the same place you were, and they are ready to give up. They feel like they are the only one going through that situation and so hearing your story will help them overcome.

Somebody else needs to know that God is a healer, that He is a deliverer, that He is a provider and He is a Savior. Someone needs to know that there is life after divorce. Someone needs to know that you can have success growing up in a broken home and that you don't have to be a drug dealer, a drug user, a pimp or a prostitute. Somebody needs to know that because your daddy left, doesn't mean you have to sleep with every Tom, Dick, and Harry who winks at you; nor do you have to hate every man that tries to come into your life.

You can't forget what God has brought you through because as was stated in a previous chapter, it's not about you! God allowed you to go through what you went through to help someone else.

Please don't forget ... Somebody's life is depending on hearing your story!

List three (3) things that are significant that God has brought you out of and delivered you from:

_____

_____

_____

_____

Are there any areas of your life that you still need healing in? Be honest because you can't get help or deliverance until you get honest. God already knows anyway.

_____

_____

_____

_____

_____

Is there anyone that you need to let go of and forgive? If so, list their name below and begin to pray and ask God to help you let it go. Whatever they did does not define you, but rather empowers you because you made it through it and now have the testimony: I made it and I am a survivor!

_____

_____

_____

_____

Chapter 10

"Work Your Stuff!"

39 And David girded his sword upon his armour, and he assayed to go; for he had not proved it. And David said unto Saul, I cannot go with these; for I have not proved them. And David put them off him.

40 And he took his staff in his hand, and chose him five smooth stones out of the brook, and put them in a shepherd's bag which he had, even in a scrip; and his sling was in his hand: and he drew near to the Philistine.

1 Samuel 17:39-40

The Power to Become

How many times have you looked at others and admired them? Perhaps you've seen someone do what you want to do and said, "I wish I could do that." Maybe you said, "If only I had their ability or their money, I could do that." The truth is, we are equipped with everything we need to accomplish our God-given destiny. Where many people mess up is when they try to be and do things like someone else.

As we look at the story of David in I Samuel 17, we see David as a confident shepherd boy with a zeal to fight the Philistine giant. When King Saul gave him the approval to go against the Philistine giant, he also provided him with his armor. Though David tried it on, he made the decision not to use it. He says, "I have not proved them." In other words, David rightly said: I haven't used this before, so I'm going to stick with what I know.

Too many times we are so infatuated with other people and their skills and ability that we forget our own skills, talents, tools, and abilities. When working to accomplish your goals, dreams, and aspirations, you have to remember to be comfortable in being yourself and doing it like God has given it to you. You may not pray like someone else prays or sing like someone else sings, but that doesn't mean your prayer or song isn't effective.

There are many ideas, inventions and projects that are in the graveyard because someone spent more time worrying about their inadequacies rather than using their strengths to effect change. If we used half the energy we use to fit in to work our purpose, we would be much further along and a lot more effective.

You must be careful about (overly) admiring someone else's gift and/or ability because you don't know what it took to produce it. If you had to go through what they went through to get it, it might kill you. And furthermore, just because it worked for them doesn't mean it's going to work for you.

I can remember some years ago when churches use to go door-to-door witnessing. We had a team that went out to a semi-rough side of town. In our group, we had people who were veteran missionaries all the way down to new converts that just wanted to tell somebody about Jesus. When we arrived at our destination, we got out of our vehicles, broke into groups of two and went out.

We noticed that some of the new converts were running to people saying, "You need to get saved or you're going to hell!" Though the few people they had approached were understanding and even receptive, the pastor at the time instructed them not to do that because it could be offensive, and people wouldn't receive them.

Well, they tried it the way the pastor had instructed them, but we then noticed their effectiveness went way down. The pastor then told them to do it however they were comfortable. They went back to their hard "in your face" militant way of doing things, and surprisingly, it worked. They won more to Christ that day than the seasoned veterans. Though it's not a recommended witnessing strategy, it worked for them at the moment, and the moment they were made to change they lost impact.

In essence, you can accomplish more working your abilities and expertise than you can trying to do it like someone else. It might be different, unconventional, unpopular and even misunderstood, but WORK YOUR STUFF!

Chapter 11

"Shut Up and Let It Speak!"

50 So David prevailed over the Philistine with a sling and with a stone, and smote the Philistine, and slew him; but there was no sword in the hand of David.

51 Therefore David ran, and stood upon the Philistine, and took his sword, and drew it out of the sheath thereof, and slew him, and cut off his head therewith. And when the Philistines saw their champion was dead, they fled.
1 Samuel 17:50-51

Hearing the title may make some say, that's a bit harsh. However, it's a truth many need to accept and embrace. Though it is human nature to desire to be liked and accepted, we have to fight the urge to compete, compare, and prove ourselves to others. This will get us in trouble every time. Doing this also causes us to get out of position and process. We enter into areas we may not be ready and prepared for, and ultimately, it backfires on us and causes us to look like a fool.

It is not our job to prove ourselves. According to Romans 8:30, who the Lord calls, He justifies and glorifies. Habakkuk 2:3 lets us know that it, referring to the vision, shall speak and not lie. No matter who doesn't like it, want it or accept it, they can't stop it if God has commanded it.

People will try to size you up by the way you look, where you come from, and what they heard about you from your past. Let them! That is none of your business. Your focus should stay on your assignment. God does not need, want, or solicit anyone's approval when He calls you and chooses to bless you. We waste too much time trying to force non-factors to see and believe what God has promised us. If God has made you a promise, all He needs is for you to come in agreement with His Word and walk out the process to attain it. That's it! That's all!

The fact that your opponent underestimates you gives you an advantage as they won't expect what's coming. When David went out to fight the Philistine, the Philistine thought it was a joke and began to laugh. He even went as far as to mock David because of his stature, but David remained focused and kept his trust in the God of his salvation. Because of David's faith and focus, he was able to triumph over Goliath and found favor in the eyes of the people and the king.

When you are anointed, called, and gifted, the results speak for themselves. You have to know that God can and will speak for Himself. Stop worrying about people and what they say. Don't allow them to pull you out of character. Some of them have aborted their babies and want you to abort and/or forfeit yours. Don't let them do it! Stay focused and keep it moving. Most importantly: Shut Up and Let It Speak!

Chapter 12

"No More Excuses!"

4 Then the word of the Lord came unto me, saying,

5 Before I formed thee in the belly I knew thee; and before thou camest forth out of the womb I sanctified thee, and I ordained thee a prophet unto the nations.

6 Then said I, Ah, Lord God! behold, I cannot speak: for I am a child.

7 But the Lord said unto me, Say not, I am a child: for thou shalt go to all that I shall send thee, and whatsoever I command thee thou shalt speak.

8 Be not afraid of their faces: for I am with thee to deliver thee, saith the Lord.

9 Then the Lord put forth his hand, and touched my mouth. And the Lord said unto me, Behold, I have put my words in thy mouth.

Jeremiah 1:4-9

How many times have we evaluated our lives and realized we have reached a certain point, and we're not as far along as we thought we would be at the current stage in our life? Maybe your life seems to be one disappointment and/or failure after another. It seems like you just can't get it right.

As we assess our lives, we recount the times we took bad advice, so called friends betrayed us, and lovers and loved ones walked out leaving us bruised, battered and torn. Perhaps our parents dropped the ball at some point in our childhood. Maybe they weren't even there, or even if they were there, maybe they weren't able to protect us or allowed us to be molested. Maybe if your friends helped you more ... they do know you're struggling.

64

Surely your family should pitch in … they say they love you. Yes, all these are good excuses, but what is it changing? Nothing!

There comes a point in our lives where we have to take ownership for our actions and the place that we are in. Though people and circumstances influence us, the fact of the matter is we are responsible for our actions and reactions. In everything that we do, we have a choice. Even if someone put a gun to your head and tells you to do something, you still have a choice.

We have potential locked inside of us to be and do whatever we desire to do and are called to do. We have to make the decision to go through the process, do the work necessary, and take responsibility for our actions and choices.

Now we are at the crossroads. What are you going to do? Are you going to continue to use the crutch that you've allowed to hold you back all these years or are you ready to put away the excuses and go get your destiny? Yes, because of circumstances and situations that arise we may have to re-route, re-vamp, and/or re-think, but we don't have to quit. It is easy to place the blame on someone else and say if they had or had not, but the truth is, all that does is give you an excuse to stay where you are. There will always be a reason to stay or to stop, but you must have the determination that where I'm going is greater than where I am, and it is worth the fight.

The truth is if you don't reach your destiny, it's nobody's fault but your own. Nobody owes you anything, and no matter what they did or didn't do, it doesn't have to stop you. Accept the fact it happened, it hurt, and you survived. Forgive and move on!

The call and promise of God does not cancel out your required work. James 2:17 (King James Version) states, "Even so faith, if it hath not works, is dead, being alone." It is my personal belief that true faith is shown through your work. If you believe that God is going to do what he promised, then you will begin to prepare for it.

For every great accomplishment, there is going to be a great obstacle. Someone once said, "Anything worth having should be worth fighting for." Most successful people have a story behind their success and a lot of the stories will leave you with your mouth hanging open.

People's opinion nor your current situation has any bearing on God's ability to bring the promise to pass. You have to make up in your mind that you are going to stop letting the hurt and pain of your past cause you to be a MESS and rather become a MESSAGE of hope and triumph.

You have to know that God has placed everything you need on the inside of you to get the job done. You have to learn to believe in yourself and the God on the inside of you. I John 4:4 states: "Ye are of God little children, and have overcome them: because greater is He that is in you, than he that is in the world." You have inside help that always get the victory.

Philippians 1:6 states that "he which hath begun a good work in you will perform it until the day of Jesus Christ." This journey is an ongoing process. You might not get there overnight but stay the course. Every journey is completed taking one step at a time. Trust in God and take that first step.

Failure is Only Solidified when you Agree with the Lie... "I Can't!"

~Larry D. Sims

BIBLIOGRAPHY

King James Version Bible – www.biblegateway.com

Definitions – www.dictionary.com

CREDITS

Book Editing by:

Rising Star Entrepreneurial Enterprises LLC
Renée Purdie, Global Brand Builder & Manager
Email: info@msrisingstar.com
Website: www.msrisingstar.com

Minister Sherika Gray

Book Cover Design by:

Kingdom Solutions Consulting & Design
Larry Sims, Owner – Designer & Branding Coach
Email: kingdomsolutionscandd@gmail.com
Website: www.kingdomsolutionsonline.com

About the Author:
Apostle Larry Donell Sims, D. Min.

Larry Donell Sims is a New Generation Apostle called to touch the Nations of the earth with an Apostolic Kingdom message of healing, deliverance, empowerment and hope. Dr. L.D. Sims has been preaching the Word of God in Power and Demonstration for more than 20 years now.

Larry Donell Sims was born to Mr. Larry and Rosa Sims on July 29, 1981 in Killeen, Texas, he was always a special child.

Apostle L.D. Sims began singing at the age of two with two of his cousins and they were called "The Faithful Few." Having a love and personal relationship with God, he received the gift of the Holy Ghost at the age of four and publicly accepted Christ at the age of six at People's Baptist Church in Montgomery, Alabama under the leadership of the late Reverend Paul L. Boswell.

Apostle Sims acknowledged his call to ministry at the age of 12 after much toil, prayer and receiving a confirming word from the late Bishop Paul White. He preached his initial sermon on October 19, 1993 at Mt. Olive Primitive Baptist Church under the leadership of Reverend Amos Williams, Sr. He was licensed as a minister on January 5, 1994 in the Mallard Creek Primitive Baptist Association.

The Power to Become

Apostle Sims was educated in the Montgomery City and Decatur City School Systems and graduated from Austin High School in Decatur, Alabama in 1999. Apostle Sims was licensed as a Prophet in 1999 by Grace & Truth Outreach Ministries. He was ordained an Elder in the Lord's Church in July of 2001. In 2005, he received a Doctorate in Ministry from St. Luke Evangelical Seminary.

In December of 2007, Apostle Sims acknowledged and accepted the Apostolic call and mandate on his life and was later affirmed an Apostle by Apostle Dr. Laura M. Thompson at Open Door Church Ministries in 2011.

In July 2016, Apostle Sims was duly consecrated to the episcopal office of Bishop in the Lord's Church and serves as Executive Board Member and North Alabama Jurisdictional Bishop for Bridging the Gap International Fellowship of Churches under the leadership of Archbishop C. W. Maddox.

He was wedded in Holy Matrimony to Lady Adrean Nicole Simmons-Sims on March 21, 2009.

Apostle Sims is the Founder and Overseer of Oasis Life Center Church International and Founder of The Kingdom Centre, an outreach established to minister to the needs of the community. He also travels this nation and abroad ministering at concerts, conferences, revivals and special events and services. He is a highly sought Preacher and Psalmist.

Apostle Sims is the Founder & Overseer of Kingdom Dominion Covenant Fellowship, a small fellowship of churches, pastors and ministers that desire fellowship, connection and accountability.

He is also the owner and operator of Kingdom Solutions Consulting & Design, a consulting & design firm that helps businesses, individuals and ministries with all their administrative, graphic and media needs.

In all that Apostle L.D. Sims does, It is his desire to see people's lives touched and transformed through the loving and saving power of Jesus Christ. He gives ALL Glory and Praise to God and acknowledges that if any good thing comes out of him, God did it!

The Power to Become

Contact Information

For a complete listing of CDs, DVDs, publications and products by Apostle Larry D. Sims, to receive updates about ministry events and conferences, or for booking and coaching information, visit www.drldsims.org or email ldsimsonline@gmail.com.

Connect with Apostle L. D. Sims on Social Media!

www.facebook.com/LDSimsOnline

www.instagram.com/LDSimsOnline

@LDSimsOnline

@LDSimsOnline

www.youtube.com/LDSimsOnline

The Power to Become

Advancing the Kingdom, Fulfilling the Mandate

What is the Kingdom Global Partnership Network?

KGPN is a group of individuals, churches, ministries, and businesses/organizations who commit to supporting and undergirding the ministry of Apostle L. D. Sims and The Kingdom Centre, Inc. by sowing a minimum seed of:

$12.00 for Individuals

$50.00 for Businesses/Churches/Ministries

This support is done through daily prayer, consistent financial support, providing needed products and services to the ministry free of charge or at a discounted rate, and supporting local and national events.

Why Join the Kingdom Global Partnership Network?

There are many reasons to join the Kingdom Global Partnership Network. There are so many people that we will encounter and have the opportunity to help that you may never see, but because of your intercession and liberal donation to this ministry you then become a part of helping those people and carrying the cause. Your continued prayers and donation(s) put you in the position to be there even though you are not physically there. So

Please Consider Helping the Cause and Become a Kingdom Expansion Partner/Sponsor TODAY!

Donations can be made with your Credit/Debit Card through our:

Website: www.DrLDSims.org

PayPal: Paypal.me/LDSM

CashApp: $DrLDSims

You can also mail a Check/Money Order made payable to: L.D. Sims Ministries, Inc.

L. D. Sims Ministries, Inc.

P.O. Box 5165

Decatur, Alabama 35601

The Power to Become

Made in the USA
Middletown, DE
19 August 2022

71082947R00050